Cover Inspiration from Sculpture Created by:
Kyle Salandy

Published by
Revolutionary Hearts Industries

Illustrated by Naomi Winston

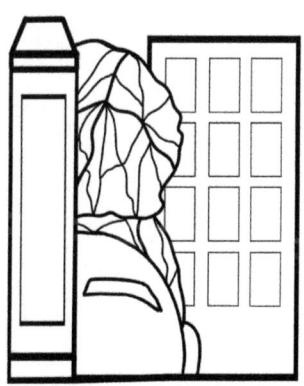

To an amazing artist,

You are the one person in your life who has the power to create your world.

I want you to take this book and be able to create your own colors to fill in the numbers. The numbers are randomly put into different shapes, so ensure to follow the numbers as best as you can when you create your color palette. (Don't be afraid to try out the challenges either!)

I remember when I first started painting or doing art I thought everything had to be perfect. I was always so scared to go over the lines when I colored but there is no fear of that here!

Go over the lines, blend your colors, and put random colors together!

This is your book.
This is your world.
This is your creativity.

Remember, that everything has a purpose and you are everything.

You are loved and you got this!

LETTER FROM THE AUTHOR

COLOR YOUR OWN WORLD

Color Your Own World
Create your own color by

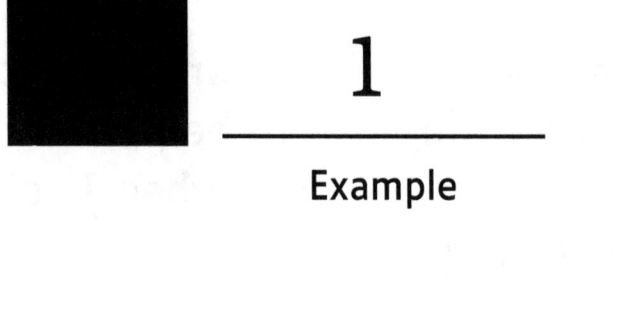

Example

** Keep an eye out for "color challenges" to stretch your creative legs! (They are optional.)

Color Your Own World
Create your own color by

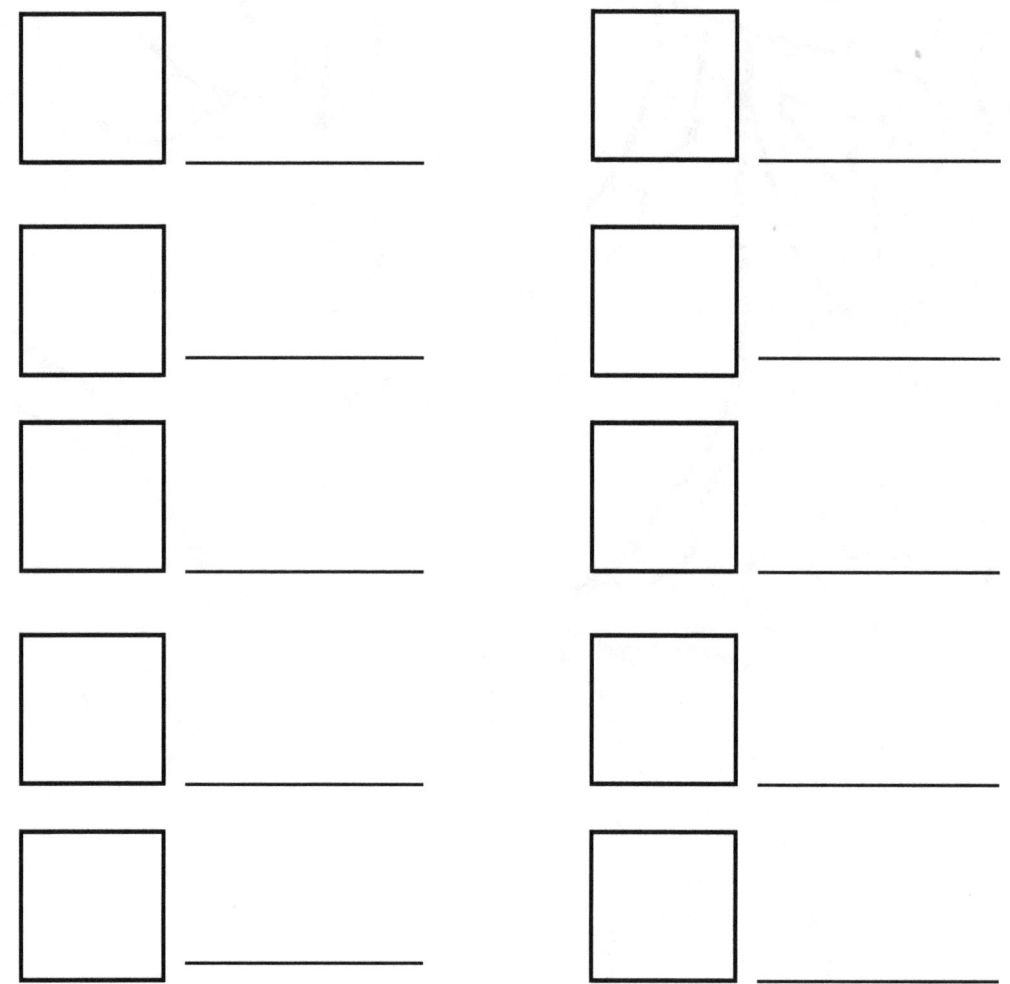

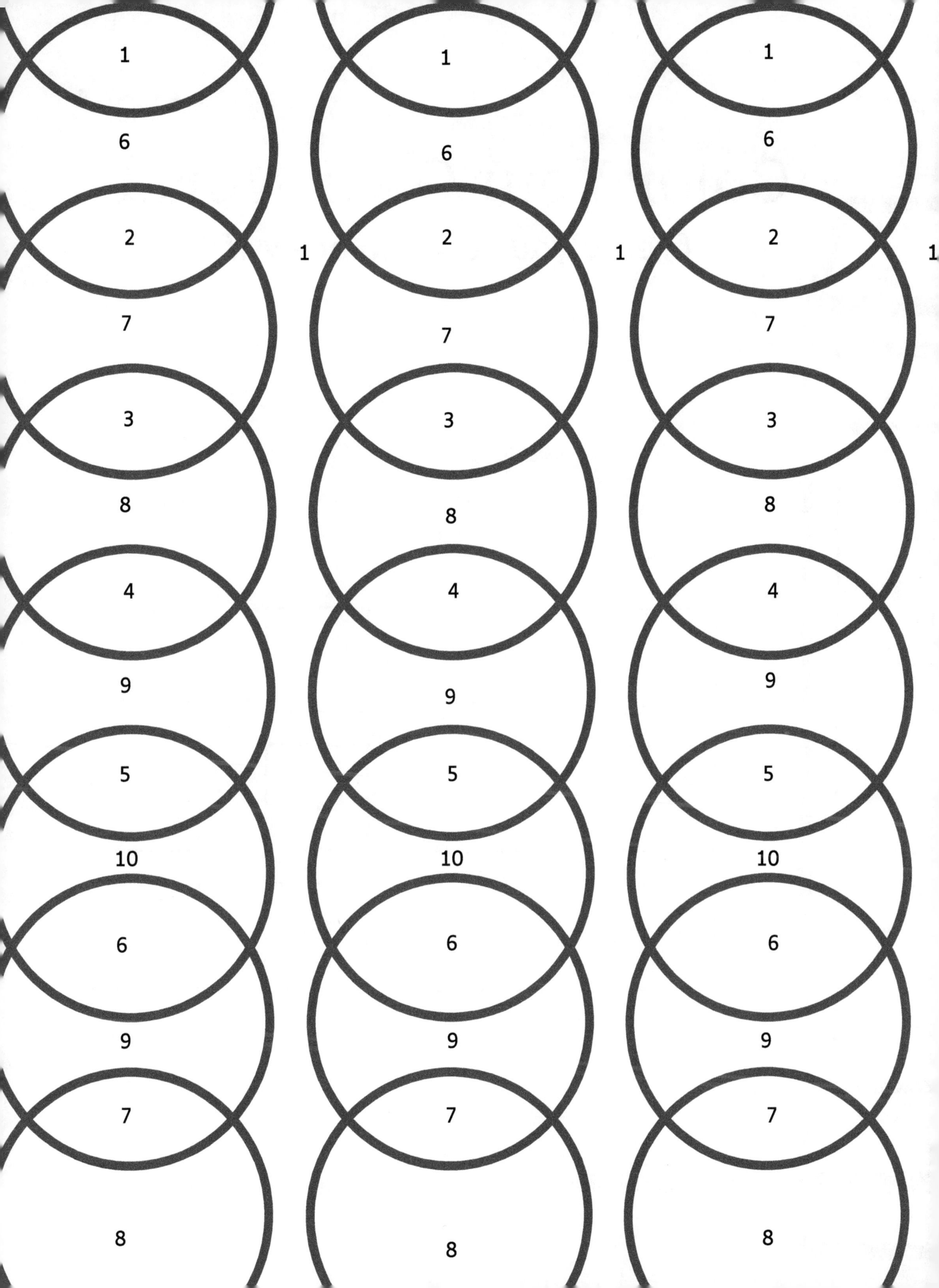

Color Your Own World
Create your own color by

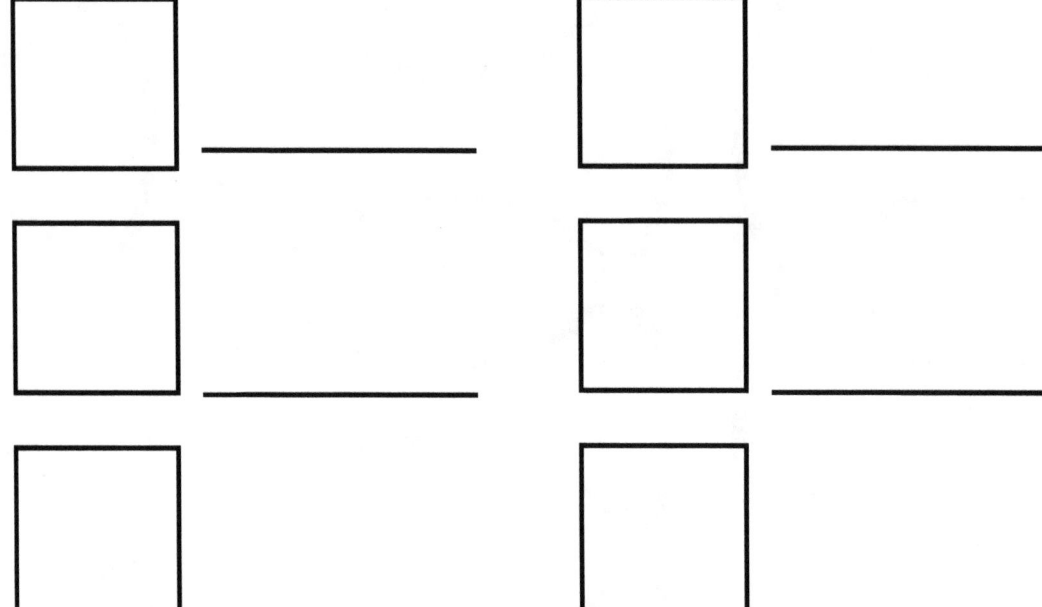

Color Challenge: Only use primary colors (shades of yellow, blue, and red)

Color Your Own World

Create your own color by

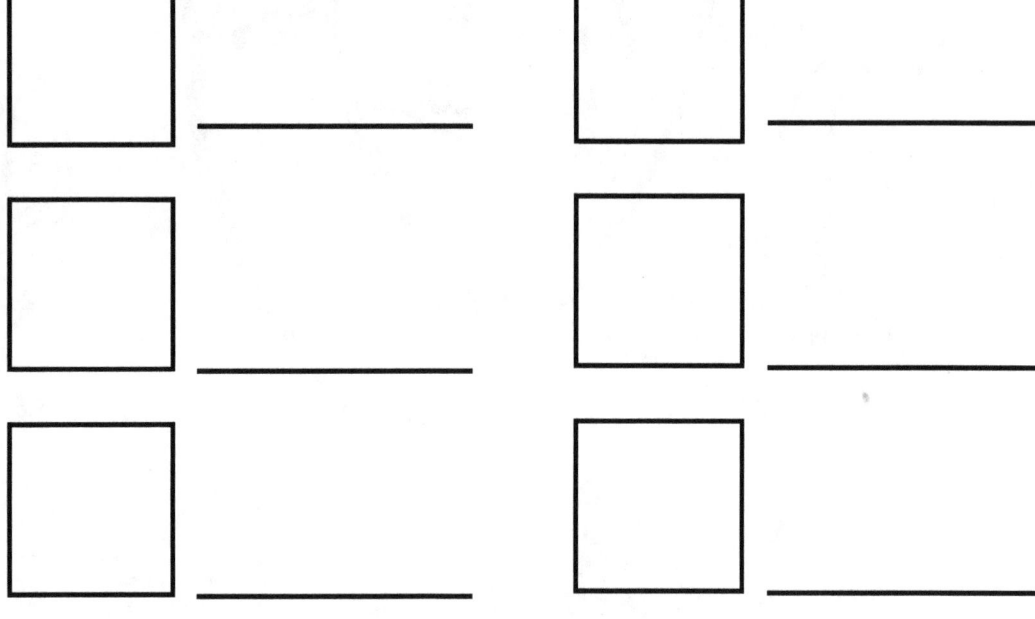

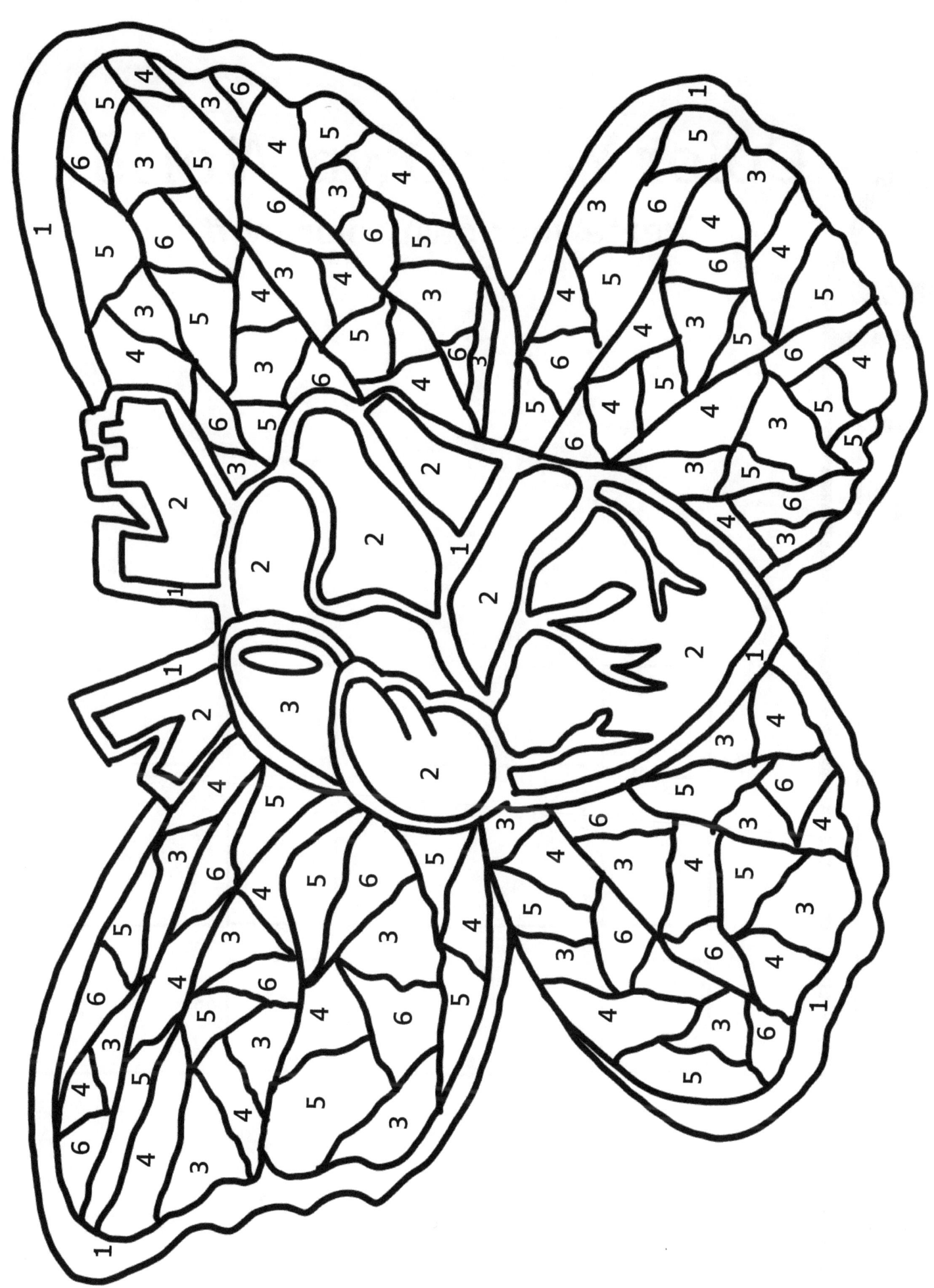

Color Your Own World
Create your own color by

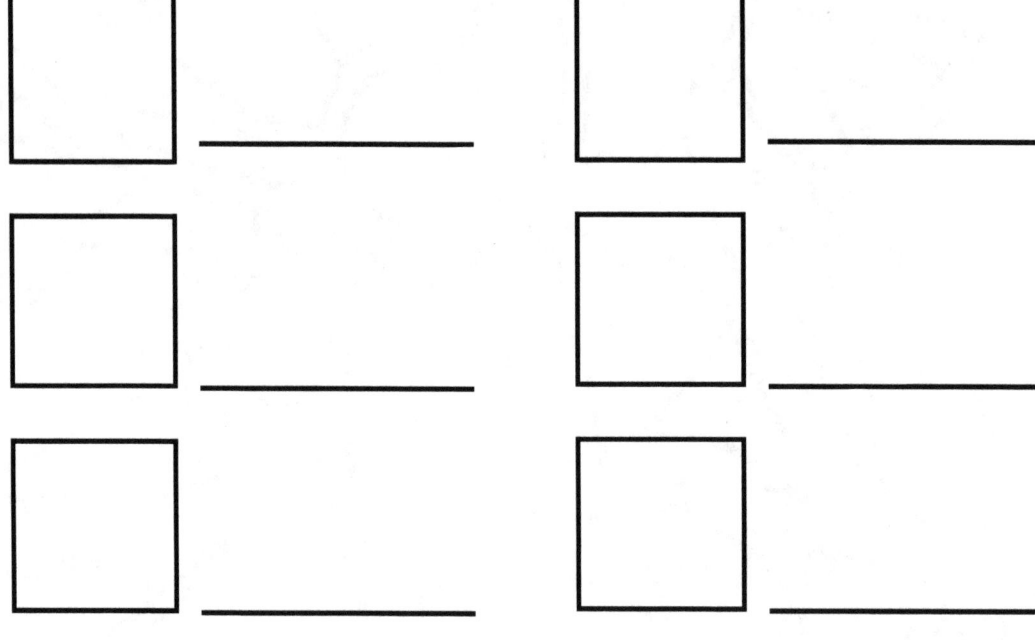

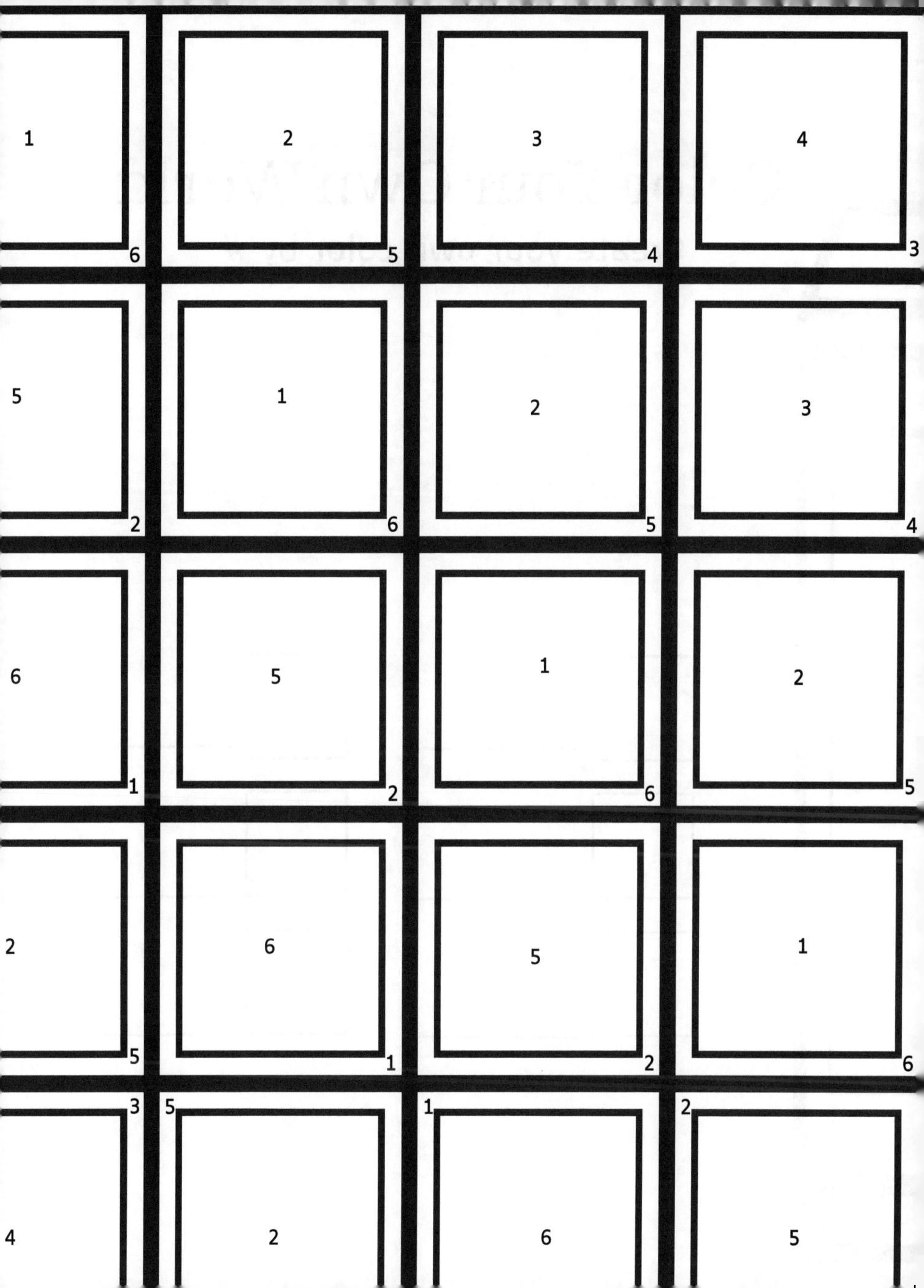

Color Your Own World
Create your own color by

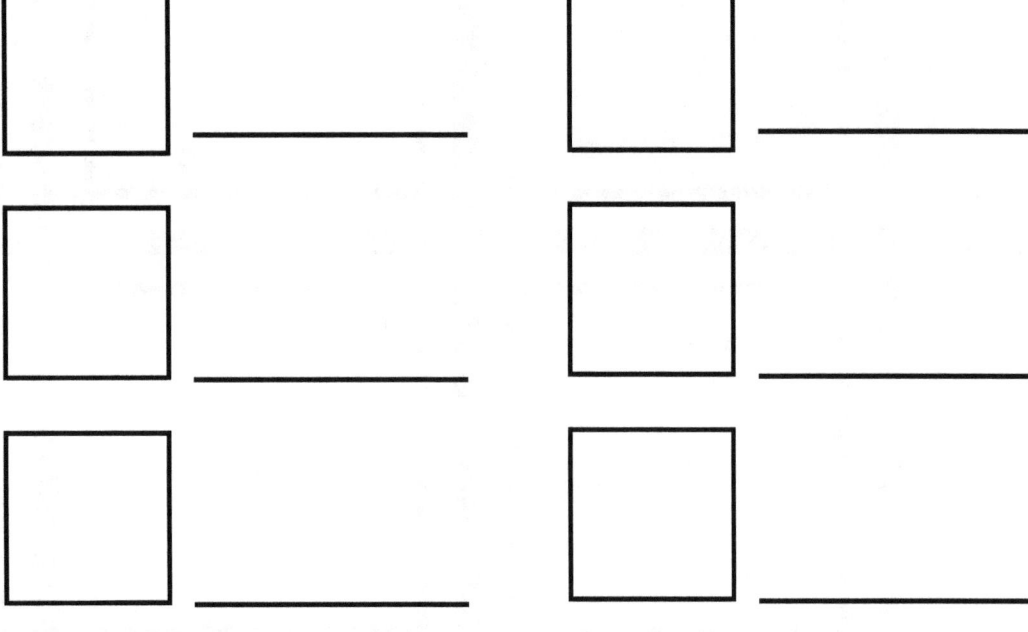

Color Your Own World
Create your own color by

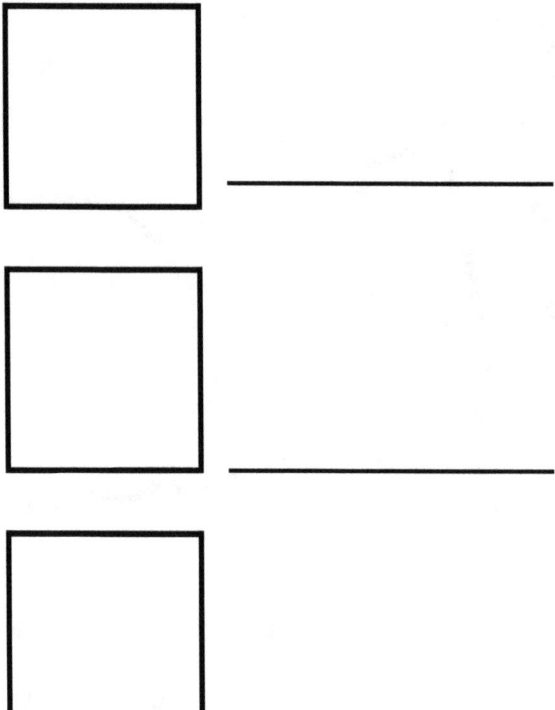

**Color Challenge: Don't use primary colors (yellow, blue, or red).

Color Your Own World

Create your own color by #

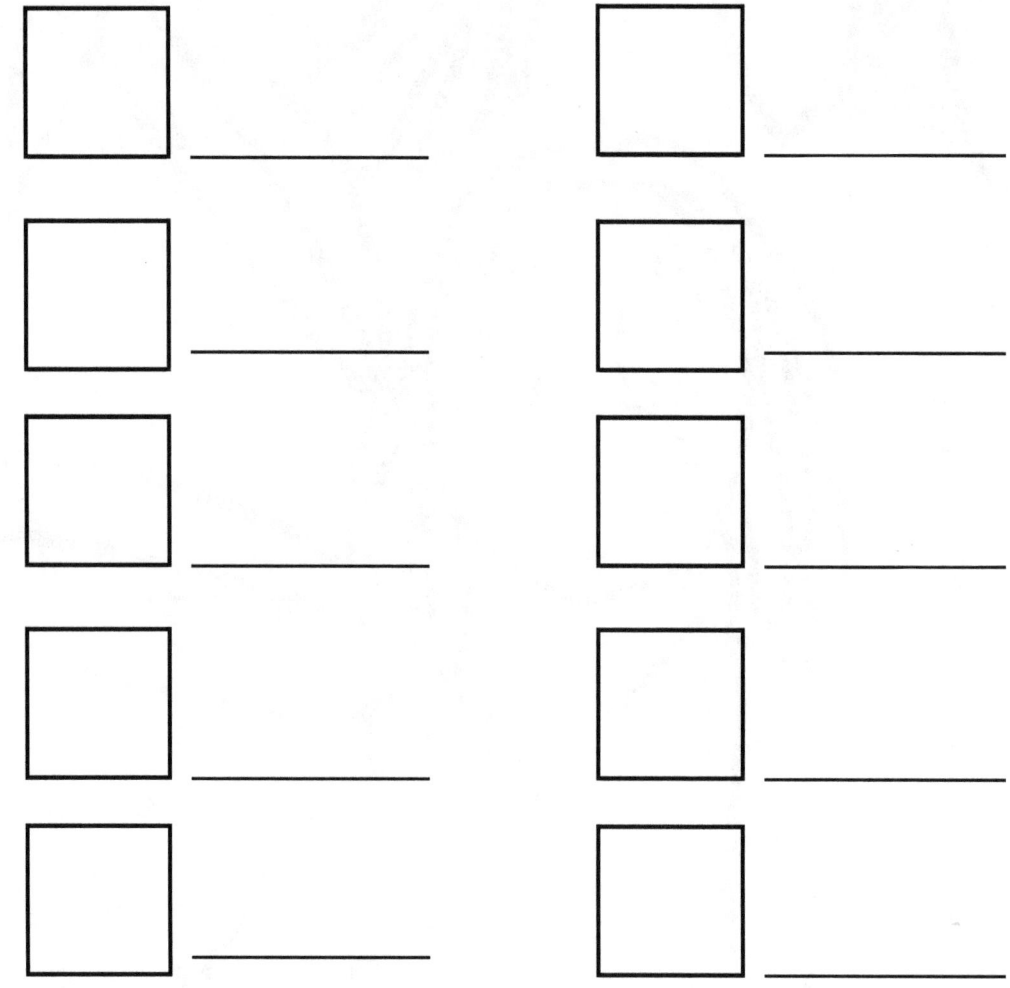

Color Your Own World
Create your own color by

**Color Challenge: Use the different shades of the same color.

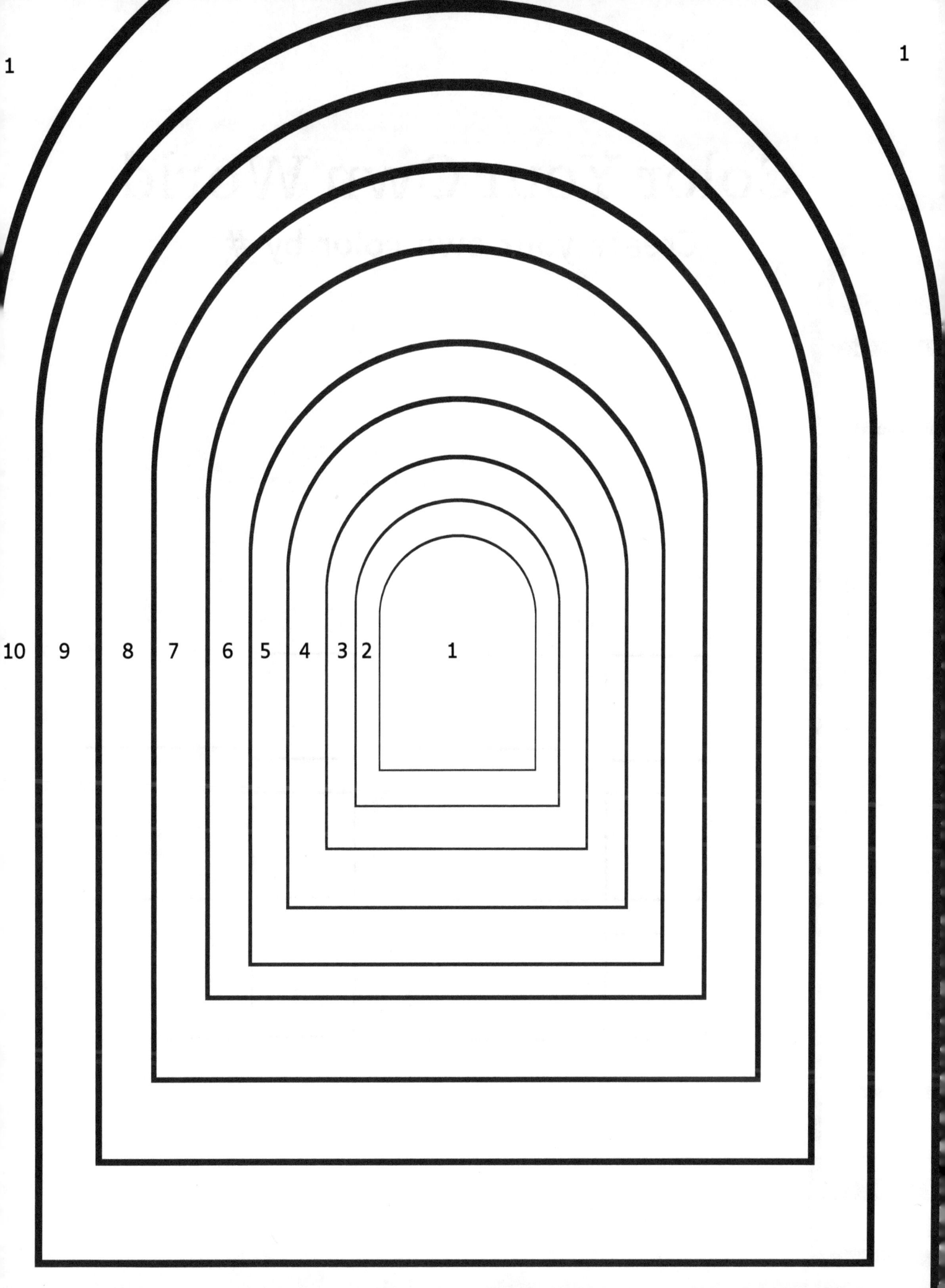

Color Your Own World

Create your own color by

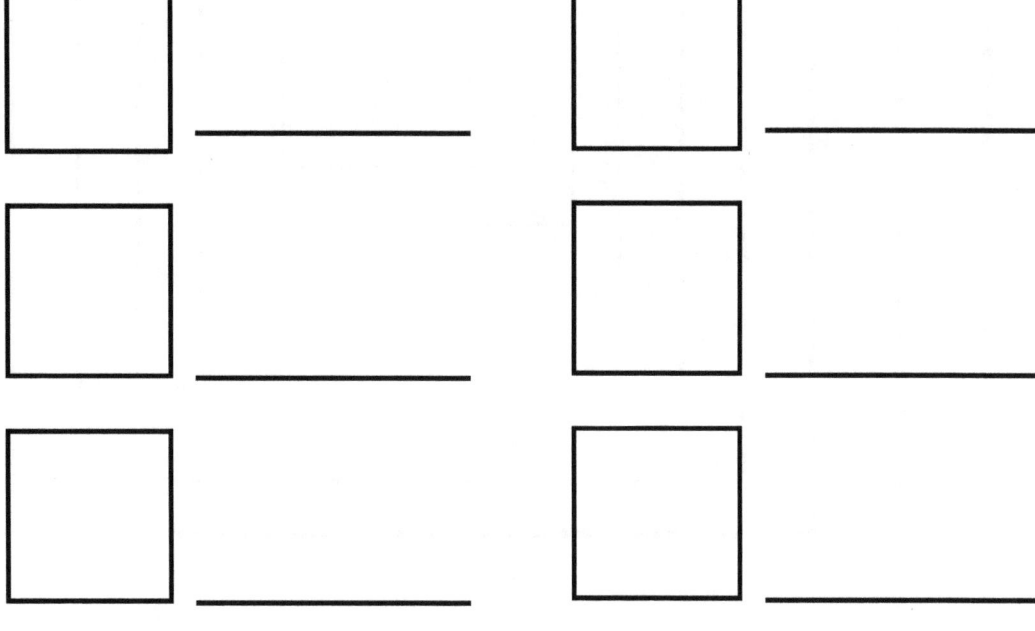

Color Your Own World

Create your own color by

**Color Challenge: Freestyle with her hair!

Color Your Own World
Create your own color by

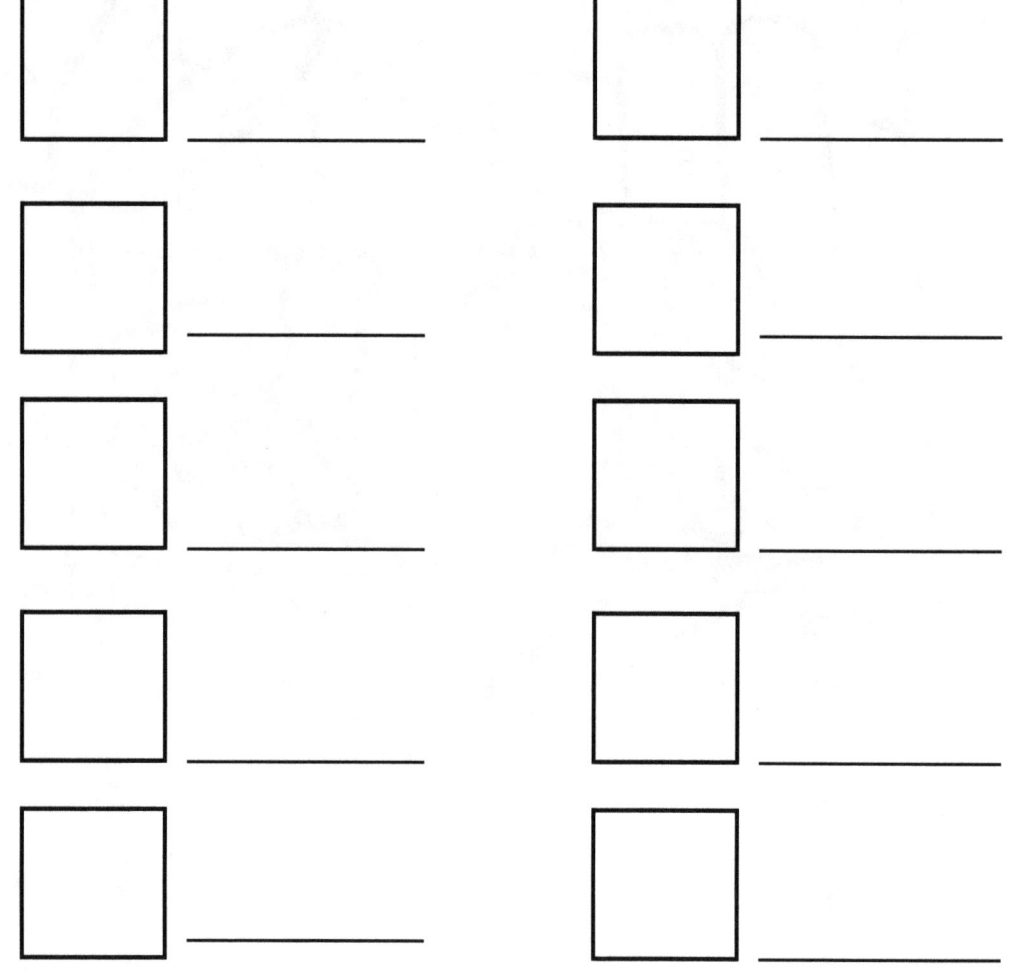

Color Challenge: Don't use any black (try other darker shades).

Color Your Own World
Create your own color by

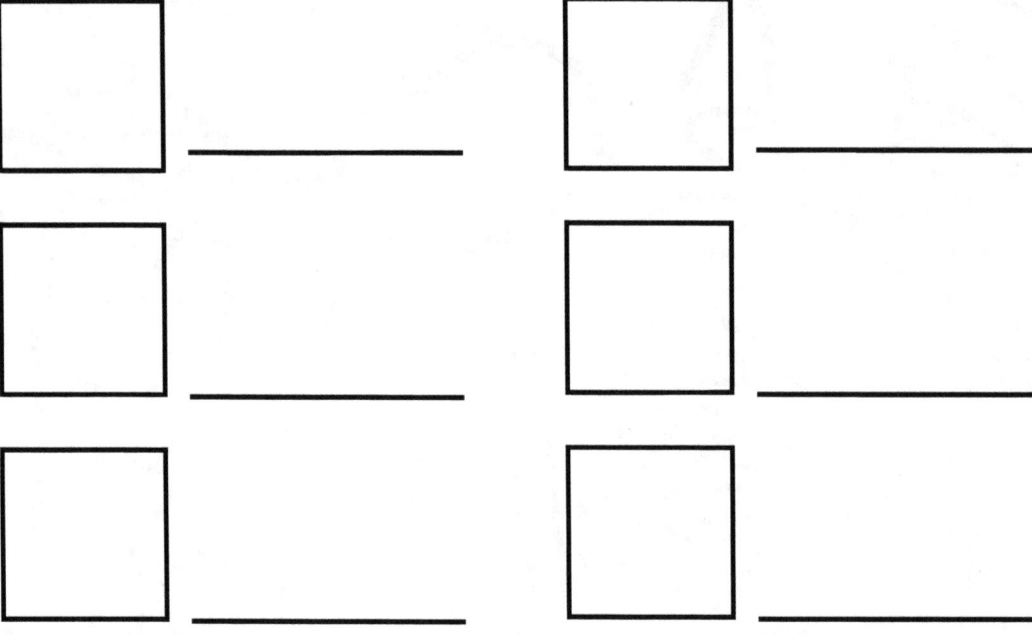

**Color Challenge: Don't use any blue.

Color Your Own World
Create your own color by

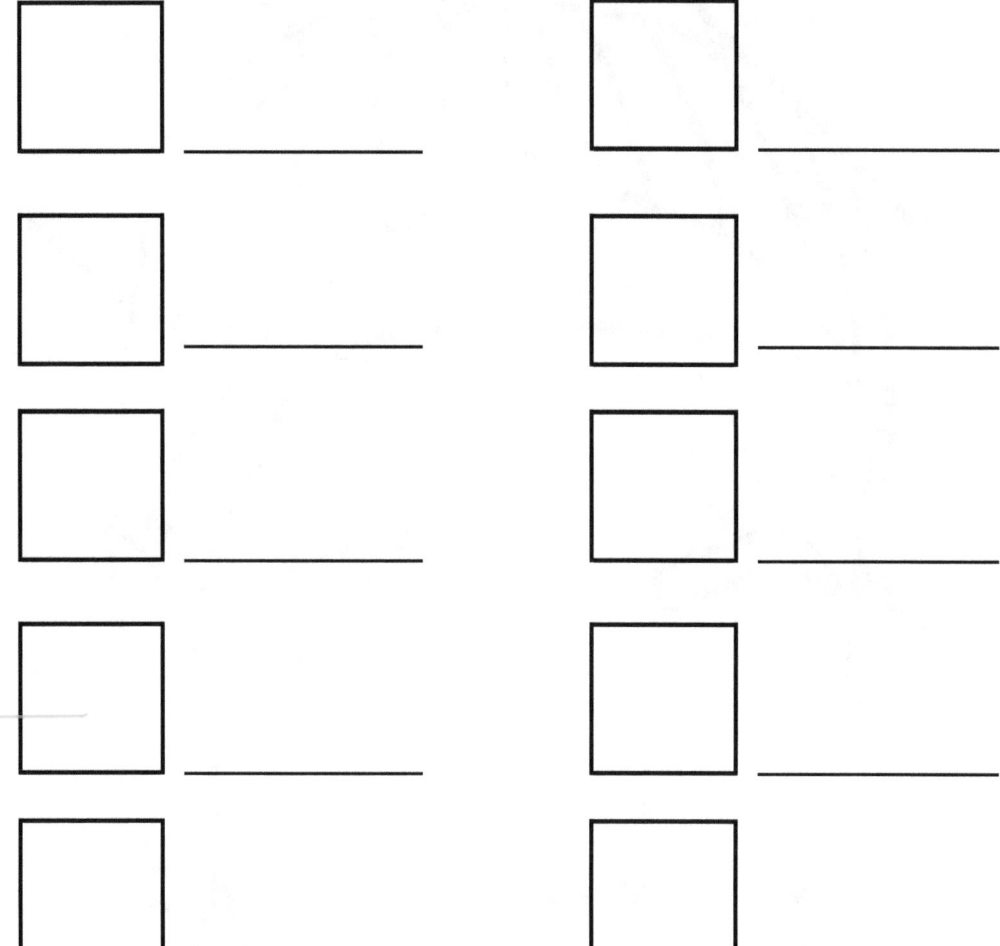

**Color Challenge: Ignore the color by # and color how you feel.

Color Your Own World
Create your own color by

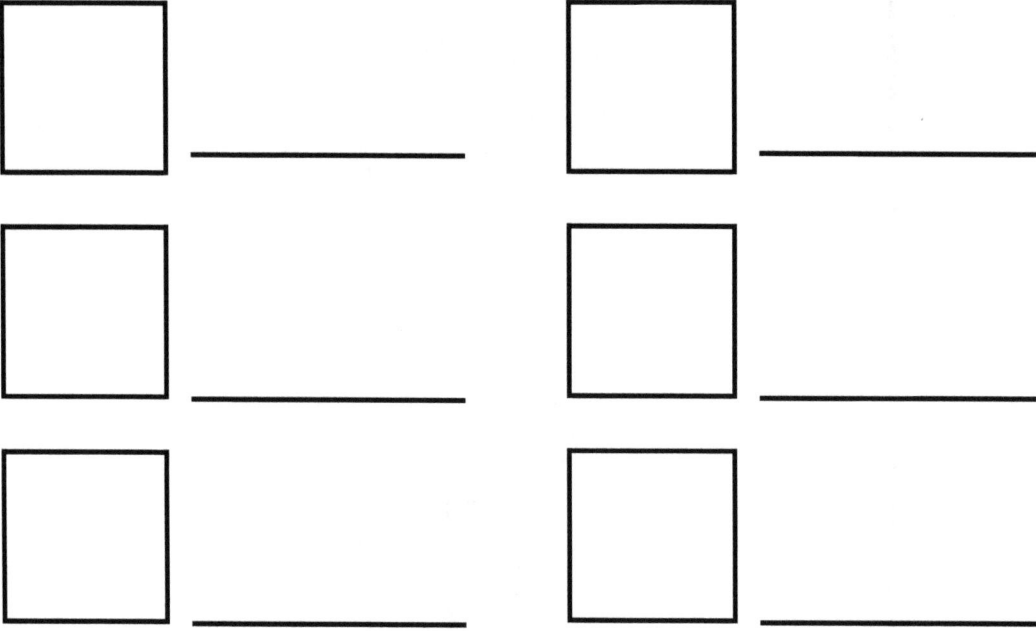

Color Challenge: Use the color that you like the least.

Color Your Own World
Create your own color by

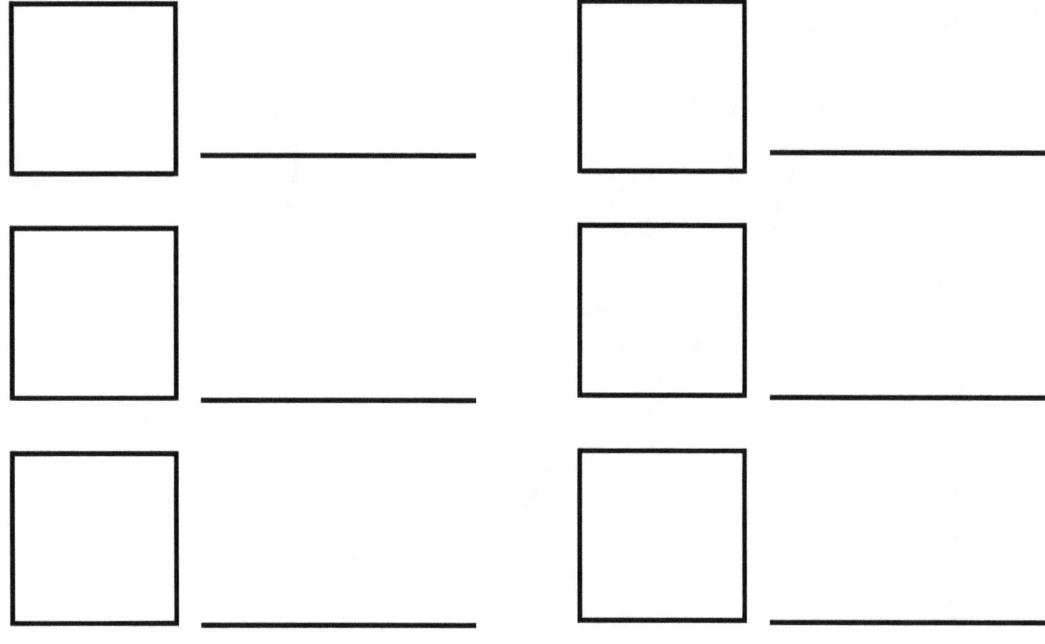

**Color Challenge: Use the side of your crayon/pencil to add texture.

Creative Representation as a Movement for Change

Naomi Winston

When I first started designing coloring books, I had no idea what I was doing! All I had was an idea and a sketch book. That was 3 years ago and now I have been able to reach kids like you all over the world.

The point is, you don't have to know what you are doing to get started. All you have to know is why you are doing it and have the grace to always continue learning even when it is hard. Growth and the willingness to learn new skills will give you more in life than anything else.

You are loved. You matter. You are everything you need to be.

I am so incredibly proud of you but don't forget to take the time to be prideful of yourself as you are growing up and growing into your passions/creativity.

Remember, everything happens for a reason and you are everything,

P.S. Some of these are past paintings and sketches of mine.

We would love to hear from you!

Email letters telling us about your passion/dreams, comments, and pictures of finished coloring pages to:

letterstotheauthor@revolutionaryheartsind.com.

We know that creating representation for Black and Brown kids means listening to their experiences, their stories, and their passions.

We would love to feature your artwork/stories!

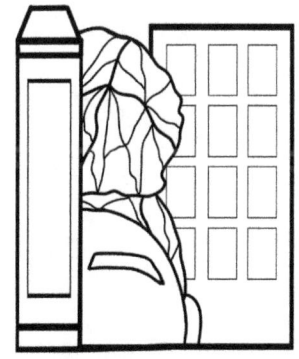

If you are interested in checking out our other coloring books make sure to go to www.revolutionaryheartsind.com

Printed in the USA
CPSIA information can be obtained
at www.ICGtesting.com
LVHW061213170924
791307LV00011B/339